The Scottish Collection

Scottish
FIRST NAMES

Julia Cresswell

HarperCollins*Publishers*

Cover image:
Lady Dorothy Dunnett, by kind permission of the owner

HarperCollins Publishers
PO Box, Glasgow G4 0NB

First published 1999

Reprint 10 9 8 7 6 5 4 3 2 1 0

© HarperCollins Publishers, 1999

ISBN 0 00 472259 0

A catalogue record for this book is available from the British Library

Printed and bound in Great Britain by The Bath Press

Contents

Introduction

Scotland has an unusually rich heritage of personal names, thanks to the wide variety of languages and cultures that have come together to form the nation. The earliest inhabitants of the land that we know anything about were the Picts and the British. Mystery surrounds the Picts, but it is known that they spoke a language that was one of the major branches of the Celtic languages, and was a form of the ancestor of modern Welsh, technically known as Brittonic. For simplicity I have called it British. It was probably spoken in certain areas up until the eleventh century, but had been replaced in most areas well before that. It left behind a number of personal names and many place names, some of which later became surnames, and some of these in turn were adopted as first names.

The reason the British language died out was that it was under pressure from two new waves of arriving settlers. From about the late fifth century the Scots from northern Ireland were crossing into Argyll. They spread out from this area, taking their language, the Gaelic branch of Celtic, and their stock names with them. These names form the bulk of what are considered as typical Scottish names. In the eastern Lowlands the peoples of the Anglian branch of the Anglo-Saxons were arriving, bringing with them their Germanic personal names. These were mostly made up of name elements of which any two could be recombined to make a new name. Certain elements would be traditional in certain families, so that someone's ancestry could be known by their

name. The combinations gradually became fixed into certain forms, such as Edward, that are still used today. The sixth-century British epic poem *The Gododdin* tells of the crushing defeat of the British inhabitants of Edinburgh when they tried to stop this advance.

From the end of the eighth century Vikings began raids on the country, and by the middle of the ninth century the northern and western isles, Caithness and Sutherland were part of a Viking-controlled region stretching from Greenland to southern Ireland. The attraction of Scotland was its mild climate and space compared with cold, over-populated Norway. To the Vikings this was the warm south, which explains why part of their territory was named Sutherland, literally 'south land'. These Vikings spoke a language called Old Norse, which was another Germanic language. The Norse influence was long-lasting; the Hebrides, for instance, only passed from Norwegian control to Scottish control in the 1460s. Meanwhile Scandinavians and Scots had intermarried and their cultures had merged, with the result that the English form of many of the Old Norse names, for example, Sorley, come by way of Gaelic rather than directly from Old Norse.

The next big influx of names came when David I, who had been brought up in the English court, came to the throne in 1124. He brought with him a following of Norman French barons, who not only introduced French culture to the country, but also new names. These came in two forms: the names they brought over with them at the time of the Norman conquest, many of which, such as Robert, were Germanic in origin and followed the same pattern as Anglo-Saxon names; and also territorial names, such as Bruce and Lindsay, which later became first names. On top of all these influences we must add the general fund of names that came with Christianity. Additionally, though in much more recent times, there are names brought in by contact with other countries or used because they had become internationally famous and fashionable.

A peculiarity of Celtic names is that many of them have anglicized equivalents, often with no apparent connection, though sometimes there is a connection through sound and meaning. In part this is because Celtic names were felt not to be Christian names, which should be those from the Bible and saints. But more important was the pressure put on Gaelic speakers by those in power to abandon their language and culture in the hope that this would make them more amenable to their loss of freedom and status. Where possible I have recorded these anglicizations.

Another particularly Scottish naming habit is a more lavish use of surnames as first names than has been common elsewhere. While I have covered some of these in this book, it is too small to attempt to do more than deal with the most common ones. Those who wish to look further into this area should turn to David Dorward's excellent *Scottish Surnames* in the Collins Pocket Reference series. Similarly, there are many names used in Irish that are occasionally found in Gaelic-speaking areas which, again because of space, are not covered here. Those interested might refer to my Collins Gem *Irish First Names*. Those interested in looking firther into Scottish names might like to start with the useful pages on the Internet sites of the General Register Office:

http://www.open.gov.uk/gros/groshome.htm

and at their list of the current most popular names:

http://roof.ccta.gov.uk/gros/names.htm#top

For those interested in the earliest Scottish names the Internet Medieval Scotland site:

http://www.abdn.ac.uk/~his016/medieval_scotland.html

will point you to a number of web-pages compiled by members of the Academy of St Gabriel on the subject.

Julia Cresswell

Adam m. Adamína f.

Although a biblical name, Adam has been in use among Gaelic speakers for over a thousand years, and is still popular today. The Gaelic spelling of the name is **Adhamh**, and there is a distinctively Scottish pet form, **Adie**, (Gaelic *Adaidh*), shared with AIDAN. The Lowlands form of the name, **Edom**, is found in the Border Ballad of *Edom O'Gordon*: 'Wha reck'd nae sin nor shame'. There is a Scottish feminine form, **Adamina**. The name **Adamnan** (**Adhamhnan**), borne by a seventh-century saint and biographer of St Colomba, may have come from Adam, but more probably comes from a word meaning 'fear'. It is sometimes anglicized **Eunan**.

Aidan m.

This is a Gaelic name, meaning 'little fire', originally a pet form of **Aoh** (see HUGH). It's most famous holder was St Aidan (d.651) who left the island-monastery of Iona to found the monastery on Lindisfarne and to convert the pagans of Northumberia. Another earlier Aidan, who died about 608, was king of the Dalriada Scots. He was crowned on Iona by St Columba himself, and thereafter fought for his kingdom's independence from the Irish Scots. Aidan is spelt **Aodán** in Gaelic, and can also be found in the forms **Aedan** and **Edan** and shares the pet form **Adie**, (Gaelic *Adaidh*) with ADAM. It is currently enjoying considerable popularity outside its native Scotland and Ireland.

Ailsa f.

There have been various suggestions as to where this name, which has been in use for over a century in

Scotland, comes from. It has been said it is a Scottish form of Elsa, or that it represents an anglicized form of **Ealasaid**, the Gaelic form of Elizabeth, but there can be little doubt that most users identify it with the name Ailsa Craig. This is a rocky island in the Clyde estuary off the Ayrshire coast. In the island's name, Ailsa comes from the Old Norse name which meant 'Alfsigr's island'. The island's name reached a wide audience as the variety name of very successful strains of tomato and onion, and may well have been taken as a personal name, as so many variety names are those of people.

Alan m.

Alan (Gaelic *Ailean*) is a Celtic name of uncertain origin and meaning. Although it is found in all the Celtic-speaking areas, it seems to have come initially from Brittany, and to have spread to the other countries by way of the Bretons who joined the Norman invasion of England. It was certainly known in Scotland in the eleventh century, when Walter fitzAlan, founder of the STUART line, was one of the Normans who accompanied King David I on his return to Scotland from England. Alan became so well-established a name that Robert Louis Stevenson could use the name in *Kidnapped* for his stereotypical quixotic Highlander, Alan Breck (There really was an Alan Breck Stewart who fought for Bonnie Prince Charlie in the Stewarts of Appin regiment, and escaped to France after Culloden. 'Breck' is a nickname meaning 'freckled'.) Scottish examples of the form ALLAN are found in Allan Ramsay (1713–1784), the portrait painter and Allan Pinkerton (1819–1884) the Scottish émigré who founded the Pinkerton Detective Agency in the USA. The feminine form **Alan(n)a** is not a Highland name, but a recent invention

Alexander m.

The ancient Greek name Alexander, 'defender of men', came to Scotland in the eleventh century, with the birth to Malcolm Canmore and St MARGARET of their fourth son, who reigned as King of Scots from 1107–24. He and his co-regent DAVID were the first kings to have non-Scottish names, and it has been suggested that Alexander was given his name by his mother who, although a descendant of the pre-Norman Conquest English kings, had been brought up in Hungary, where the medieval romances based on the life of Alexander the Great were very popular. Another Alexander, Alexander I's grandson, ruled 1214–49, and was followed by Alexander III (1249–86), giving a period of over 70 years with an Alexander on the throne, so it is hardly surprising that Alexander became a well-established Scottish name. **Sandy** (Gaelic *Sandaidh*) was the standard pet form of the name, although it could also be shortened to **Sawn(e)y** (as in the notorious fourteenth-century robber and cannibal Sawney Bean). **Saunders**, occasionally found as a first name, is usually a re-use as a first name of a surname, but was originally another pet form. **Allie** and **Al(l)y** are now common short forms. In Gaelic Alexander became **Alistair** (also **Alasdai**r, **Alastair**, **Alaster**, **Alister**), shortened to **Alick** (Gaelic *Ailig*) and **Alec**. Feminine forms of Alexander are now so common world wide that it is difficult to distinguish which ones are particularly Scottish, but unusual feminine forms found in Scotland include **Alexina**, **Alickina** and **Alina**.

Alpin m.

Alpin (Gaelic *Ailpein*) or Alpine was the name of a number of Pictish kings, but is best known today from the surname MacAlpine. It's most famous bearer was Kenneth MacAlpin ('son of Alpin'), king of the Dalriada Scots who conquered the Picts and made himself king of all the lands north of the Forth in 843, thus laying the foundations of what became the kingdom of Scotland.

Andrew *m.*

As the patron saint of Scotland, St Andrew's name has long been popular, and is still very much so today. **Dand**, **Dandy** or **Dandie** are Scottish short forms of the name, and **Drew** is also used. **Aindrea** and **An(n)dra** are Gaelic forms of Andrew, which has developed into the surname and first name Gillanders, 'servant of (St) Andrew', from the Gaelic *Gille Ainndreis* or *Gille Anndrais*.

Angus *m.*

Angus (Gaelic *Aonghus* or *Aonghas*) is an ancient Celtic name meaning 'unique choice one', and was originally the name of one of the Irish pagan gods. It is one of the earliest Gaelic names in Scotland for, according to tradition, the brothers FERGUS, Angus and LORNE were Scots who settled in Dalriada (roughly the part of the Scottish mainland nearest Ireland) about 500 AD. The Gaelic pronunciation of the name has also appeared in the form **Innes**, and this pronunciation explains why the names was 'translated' by the classical name **Aeneas** (sometimes spelt **Eneas**). The feminine forms **Angustina** and **Angusina** have been recorded.

Annabel *f.*

Annabel is now so widely found in the English-speaking world that it is difficult to remember that it was once confined to Scotland. Its history is not clear, but since it was in use by the twelfth century, when Anne was not used as a first name, it does not appear to have developed from it. It is probably a variant of **Amabel**, from the Latin *amabilis* 'loveable', which elsewhere developed into Mable. It is sometimes used to 'translate' **Barabal**, the Gaelic form of Barbara. **Arabel**, which also is a Scottish name, probably developed from the same name, but its history is further confused by the fact that early examples of the name, which are also found from the twelfth century, are usually spelt in forms such as *Orabilia*, or *Orable*, as if they cam from the Latin *orabilis* 'easily entreated'.

Archibald *m.*

Archibald is in origin a Germanic name formed from elements meaning 'genuine' and 'bold'. It became popular in Scotland and was often shortened to **Archie**, **Archy**, **Airchie** (Gaelic *Eair(r)dsidh*) or **Baldie**, because it was used to 'translate' the Scottish name **Gillespie** (Gaelic *Gilleasbaig*), meaning 'servant or devotee of the bishop'. The reason for this is obscure. It has been suggested that Gaelic speakers would be familiar enough with English to connect the '-bald' element of the name, originally meaning 'bold', with the fact that Gaelic *gille* means not only someone dedicated to a saint or member of the church, hence servant, but also, by implication, someone with tonsured hair, hence 'bald', with a possible further connection made between 'arch-bishop' and the Gaelic for 'bishop' for the first part of the 'translation'. Readers are free to draw their own conclusions.

Athol *m.*

Athol (sometimes **Atholl**) is a first name which comes

from a place name in Perthshire. The original form of the name Gaelic *ath Fodla* means 'new Ireland', a grandiose name which would have been given to the place by early Irish settlers, although in legend the name has an even grander origin, Fodla being one of the names (all linked to placenames) ascribed to the seven sons of Cruithne (the Gaelic form of the word 'Pict') who heads the traditional list of Pictish kings.

Aulay *m.*

Aulay (Gaelic *Amhla(i)dh*) is the Gaelic form of the Scandinavian name Olaf (also the source of the name Oliver), which was introduced into the Hebrides by Viking settlers.

Bean m. Beathag f.

Bean (Gaelic *Beathan*) comes from the Gaelic *beatha* 'life', and was the name of a Scottish saint of the eleventh century. An old name related to it was **MacBeth** 'son of life', which was used in a religious sense to mean 'chosen one'. It is now only found as a surname thanks, of course, to the notoriety of Shakespeare's protagonist. Bean was often anglicized as Benjamin, while **Beathag**, the feminine form, was for no particularly clear reason anglicized as Sophia or Rebecca. The comparative popularity of the unusual biblical name **Bethia** in Scotland in the past may have been because it was thought to echo Beathag.

Blair m.

This is a Scottish surname used as a first name. The surname would originally have been given to someone who lived on or by a *blar*, the Gaelic word for 'field, plain', often referring to a battle field. It is well-used by Scottish parents today.

Bonnie f.

Although the word 'bonnie', which means 'fair, beautiful' is thought of as a particularly Scottish word, the name is not a Scottish invention, but a recent American creation. A great deal of its popularity is due largely to its use in Margaret Mitchell's novel *Gone with the Wind* (1939). Although it was in use before then, as is shown by the name of Bonnie Parker of Bonnie and Clyde fame. **Blythe**, 'happy', which is a word often linked with bonnie in traditional verse, is occasionally found as a female name.

Brenda f.

This was originally a Shetland first name, probably a female version of the Scandinavian Brand, meaning 'a sword'. It came into more general use after Sir Walter Scott used it for one of the heroines of his 1821 novel *The Pirate*. In Ireland it is used as a feminine form of Brendan.

Bruce m.

The family of King Robert the Bruce (Robert I) probably took its name from the French village of Brix near Cherbourg. Although other places, such as Le Brus near Calvados and Briouze in Orme, have also been suggested. The first Robert Bruce was among the forces of William of Normandy when he invaded England in 1066. The second of that name was one of the Norman barons who accompanied David I to Scotland when he took the throne. The 8th holder of the name became king himself, having defeated the English at Bannockburn in 1314. The name does not seem to have been used as a first name until the twentieth century, but by mid-century it had become so popular in Australia that it became a term for an Australian male.

Callum *m.*

Callum or **Calum** (either spelling can be used, though Callum is perhaps marginally the more popular form of the two at the moment) is a form of the name of St Columba (521–597), whose name came from the Latin for 'dove'. The name was popular among Irish monks because it symbolized their rejection of the pagan life of strife and war for the Christian way of peace and love, which was a change Columba found difficult. After having taken part in a battle where he was badly wounded, Columba left his native land and sailed for Scotland, to be a missionary to the pagan people there. He settled on the Hebridean island of IONA, and from their his influence spread throughout Scotland. The Irish form **Colm** is occasionally found in Scotland. MALCOLM is a development of the name.

Cameron *m.*

Cameron is a Scottish clan and surname used as a first name. It is currently popular both in Scotland and the United States, where it is increasingly used for girls. The name is traditionally thought to have come from an ancestor who had a crooked nose, *cam sron* in Gaelic. More prosaic people have suggested that 'crooked nose' refers to some feature of the landscape, from which the clan took its name.

Campbell *m.*

A Scottish clan and surname, increasingly being used as a first name, from the Gaelic *cam beul*, 'crooked mouth'. According to tradition, a nickname of Gillespic O Duithne, who lived in the early thirteenth century.

Catriona *f.*

This form of the name Catherine, anglicized from Gaelic **Ca(i)triona**, became famous after R.L.Stevenson used it for Catriona Drummond, beautiful and high-spirited heroine of his 1893 novel *Catriona*, the sequel to *Kidnapped*. It is sometimes found in the form **Catrina**, either of which can be spelt with a K. Other Gaelic names from Catherine are **Ceit** (Kate) and **Ceiteag** (Katie). Catriona is quite well used in Scotland at the moment, but the Irish form Caitlin (sometimes in the form Caitlyn) is even more popular.

Clyde *m.*

Although not particularly common in Scotland, it is considerably more popular in the United States and West Indies. Clyde is, of course, the name of the great river that flows through Glasgow (compare KELVIN). It is a very ancient name, which was recorded in Roman times, and probably means 'the one who cleans', perhaps a reference to the power of the water flow. It has been suggested that the name was actually that of a river goddess, worshipped locally, but this is less generally accepted than in the past.

Coll *m.*

Coll is an early Irish name meaning 'chief, high'. According to legend, it was a name shared by three brothers who lived in Scotland for some time before winning a great kingdom for themselves in Ireland. The name was popular among the McDonalds, and the surname McColl, 'son of Coll', comes from a branch of the McDonalds.

Cosmo *m.*

A name adapted from the Italian name Cosimo 'order', may seem surprising in a list of Scottish names, but it has been in use since the eighteenth century, when it was born by the 3rd duke of Gordon. He had been given the name in honour of his father's friend, Cosimo III, Grand Duke of Tuscany. The name became traditional in the Gordon family, and from there spread to other Scottish families. A famous twentieth-century holder was Cosmo Gordon Lang, Archbishop of Canterbury 1928–1942.

Craig *m.*

This Scottish word for 'crag' was first a place name that became a surname, which in turn became a first name. Its use seems to be twentieth century, and it is currently a popular name in Scotland.

C

David m. Davina f.

This biblical name, meaning 'beloved', became a Scottish name because it belonged to two long-reigning kings: David I (1107–1153) and David II (1328–1371). David I was also one of the greatest landholders in England, and one of the most powerful barons in the English court where he grew up. His English upbringing meant that when he came to power in Scotland he brought with him not only many Norman customs, but also a number of Norman barons such as de Bailleul, fitzAlan (whose family name was later to become Stewart or STUART from their hereditary post of King's Steward) and de Bruse (later BRUCE). All families that were later to have such an influence on both the history and the names of Scotland. The normal pet form of David in Scotland was **Davie** (or **Davy**), the form more often used for David Balfour, the priggish hero of Stevenson's *Kidnapped*; while the Gaelic form is **Daibhidh**, shortened to **Daidh** (anglicized **Day** or **Dey**) or sometimes **Dàthaidh**. There are at least four Scottish feminine forms of the name in use by the seventeenth century: **Davina** (shortened to **Vina**), **Davida** (shortened to **Vida**) and the less common **Davinia** and **Davidina**. The first two of these have enjoyed some popularity outside Scotland.

Devorgilla f.

This is the English and Latin form of the Gaelic name **Diorbhail** (earlier **Diorbhorguil**), also anglicized as **Dervorguilla** and **Devorguilla**. The name was often 'translated' as Dorothy. The most famous holder of the name was Devorguilla of Galloway, daughter and heiress to Alan, the last Celtic Lord of Galloway, great-great granddaughter of King David I and mother of John de

Balliol, King of Scots (1292–96), who was nicknamed
'Toom Tabard' (Empty Jacket) after he was stripped of
his royal insignia and throne by Edward I of England.
His claim to the throne came through her. Dervorguilla
was the founderess of Sweetheart Abbey,
Kirkcudbrightshire, and is regarded as the founderess of
Balliol College, Oxford, started by her husband
apparently in penance after a quarrel with the Bishop of
Durham, but endowed by her. Because of her Oxford
connection, the name has occasionally been used outside
Scotland for the daughters of those who went to Balliol.

Donald *m.*

Donald is one of the very earliest Celtic names, a version
of it being recorded as the name of a British prince on a
Roman inscription of 20 AD, and forms of the name,
which means 'world ruler', are found in all Celtic
languages. In Gaelic the name is **Domhnall**, shortened
to **Donaidh** (**Donnie**) or **Dolaidh** (**Dolly**), while in
Ireland it takes the form **Donal(l)**. In the past the name
was so popular in the Highlands that it was used as a
generic term for a Highlander. The great MacDonald
clan, headed by the Lords of the Isles, were descendants
of Donald, grandson of the twelfth-century King
Somerled of the Western Isles. A large number of
feminine forms of the name recorded in the Highlands,
which include **Donalda**, **Donaldina**, **Donella**, **Donalla**,
Dolina, **Donelle** (primarily in Ireland), with the Gaelic
forms **Donna(g)**, **Dol(l)ag** and **Doileag**.

Dougal *m.*

Dougal, **Dugal** or **Dugald** is in Gaelic **Dubhghall** or
Dùghall, meaning 'dark stranger'; a term originally used

of Viking invaders. It is said that it referred specifically to Danish Vikings, while the blonder Norwegians and Icelanders were FINGAL, 'fair strangers'. Whatever the truth in this tradition, the name was in early use amongst the people of mixed Gaelic and Viking descent in the north and west of Scotland, and soon came to be thought of as a native Gaelic name. The Dougal who gave his name to the MacDougalls was the eldest son of King Somerled (Sorley) of the Isles. The name can be shortened to **Dougie**, and unusually for a Highland name, does not seem to have developed any feminine forms.

Douglas *m.*

The House of Douglas was one of the most prominent in Scottish history. The family fortunes were founded by Sir James Douglas (c.1286–1330), known as the Black Douglas from his dark complexion. He was a faithful follower of the Bruce whose real-life exploits in the War of Independence rivalled anything in heroic fiction. In the fourteenth century the family, now headed by an earl, was one of the greatest landowners in southern Scotland and could raise thousands of experienced men to fight against English border raiders, or to indulge in some raiding themselves. The family split into four main branches, which were often at odds with each other. In the sixteenth century, the Earl of Angus, head of the Red Douglases (named after a red-haired founder) virtually held the boy-king James V prisoner, and ruled in his name. In the same century the surname began to be used as a first name, often for girls, although there is also a rare feminine form **Douglasina**. The name was taken by Scottish emigrants to Canada and the USA, where it became very popular in the earlier part of the twentieth century, often shortened to **Doug** or **Dougie**. Ultimately, the surname comes from a Celtic place name *dubh glas* 'black stream', a name found in the Southern Uplands of Scotland where the family was originally based.

Duff *m.*

The surname Duff, sometimes found as a first name, came from the same Gaelic word *dubh*, meaning 'dark, black', as is found in DOUGAL and DOUGLAS.

Duncan *m.*

Duncan is the anglicized form of the Gaelic name **Donnchadh**, meaning 'brown warrior' (the 'brown' probably referring to hair or skin colour). The name is known worldwide as the name of the murdered king in Shakespeare's *MacBeth*, but while it can be found outside Scotland, it has never been as popular as some other Scottish names. It is, however, still well used in Scotland. Shakespeare's Duncan was a real eleventh-century king, who was already king of the Strathclyde Britons when he became the successful claimant to the throne of his grandfather Malcolm II, ruler of the Picts, Scots and Lothian Angles, who had died without sons to succeed him. Duncan thus became ruler of nearly all of modern Scotland, as well as of a large portion of what is now England. In 1040 Duncan was defeated and killed in battle by a rival claimant, Macbeth, who was in turn killed, after a successful reign, by Duncan's son Malcolm at the battle of Lumphanan in Aberdeenshire in 1057.

D

Effie *f.*

This is a pet form of the name **Euphemia**, from the Greek meaning 'fair speech', which was used in Scotland from the twelfth century onward, and was more common there than in other countries. The reason for this was that it anglicized the Gaelic **Oighrig**, a name of uncertain meaning, possibly 'new speckled one'. Oighrig, which was also anglicized as **Erica**, also took the forms **Eithrig** and **Eiric**, and in the past also Africa and Efric. As well as appearing most frequently as **Effie**, **Euphemia** could also appear as **Eppie**, **Phemie** or even **Fanny**, as well as being spelt **Euphame**.

Eilidh *f.*

Eilidh is the Gaelic form of Helen, originally a Greek name meaning 'bright one'. It is currently the most popular Gaelic name for girls in Scotland. Most non-Gaelic speakers pronounce it to rhyme with Hayley.

Elspeth *f.*

Elspeth, also found as **Elspet**, is a Scottish form of the name Elizabeth. It is found in various forms throughout the Christian world because it was the name of the mother of John the Baptist. It comes originally from the Hebrew meaning 'God has sworn'. Elspeth is shortened to **Elsie** and **Elspie**. The Gaelic forms of the name are **Elisaid** or **Elasaid**.

Eoin *m.*

This is a Gaelic form of the name John. It is the form used for saints' names, but is also used as a given name, when it tends to by anglicized as Jonathan. See Iain.

Erskine m.

This is a surname which is sometimes used as a first name. It comes from a place name near Glasgow.

Esme, Esmé(e) m. & f.

The first recorded bearer of the name Esmé was Esmé Stewart, 6th Seigneur d'Aubigny. (1542–83). He was born in France of a French mother, which may explain his name. It comes from the French for 'esteemed' but was often spelt **Aymie**, or **Aimé**, as if from the French for 'loved' (source of the girl's name Amy). Esmé Stewart was a cousin and a favourite of King James VII who made him Duke of Lennox and Lord High Chamberlain of Scotland. The name spread to other Scottish families, and from there to general use. It is often spelt **Esme** without the accent. Because it looks like a girl's name, it is now mainly used for girls, in which case it can be found in the forms **Esmée**, **Esmee** and even **Esma**.

Etta f.

Although Etta is a widely used pet form for girls' names ending -etta, in Scotland it has a special role as a pet form of Mairead (see MARGARET), which was often anglicized as **Marietta** or **Maretta**.

Euan m.

Euan is currently the most popular spelling of the boy's name which comes from the Gaelic name **Eòghann**. The spelling **Ewan** is only slightly less popular, and forms such as **Ewen**, **Euen** and even **Evan** are also found. The Irish (and Welsh) form **Owen** has recently become popular in Scotland as well. The history of the name is somewhat obscure. Not only has Euan sometimes been confused with EOIN; and been translated as HUGH, which has muddied the waters, but the origin of Eòghann is also debated. It has been claimed that it means 'son of the yew' and is a relic of ancient tree worship, or that it comes from *eoghan*, 'youth', but most commentators now accept it as a form of the name **Eugene**, meaning 'well-born, noble'.

e

Farquhar *m.*

This name, also found as a surname, comes from the Gaelic **Fearchar**, meaning 'dear man, very dear one'. A Fearchar was king of the Dalriada Scots in the seventh century. The name is used in both Ireland and Scotland, but is most common in the Highlands.

Fenella *f.*

Fenella is the anglicized spelling of the Gaelic name **Fionnghal** (Irish **Fionnuala**), 'white shoulder'. It is also found as **Finel(l)a**, **Finola** and **Fionola**, while in Ireland **Nuala** is a very popular short form. Finola MacDonnell was the Scottish mother of the Red Hugh O'Donnell, one of the most successful Irish fighters against English rule in the seventeenth century, and is said to have been the driving force behind him. Flora MacDonald who helped Bonnie Prince Charlie 'over the sea to Skye' was probably another bearer of the name, for **Flora** was the form regularly used to translate the name. She was also known as Florence MacDonald, and sometimes signed her name Florie. As a result of her fame, Flora became a popular Scottish name, with **Florrie** used as a short form, and a Gaelic spelling **Flòraidh**. The actress Fenella Fielding has made Fenella more widely known outside Scotland.

Fergus *m.*

According to legend Fergus MacErc, also known as Fergus Mor, whose name meant 'supreme choice', along with his brothers ANGUS and LORNE, led the Scots from Ireland to Dalriada, founding the Scottish kingdom there in about 500 AD. Another famous Fergus was Prince of

Galloway in the twelfth century. The name takes the form **Fearghas** in Gaelic, and has the pet form **Fergie**.

Fife *m.*

Legend says that the Scottish district of Fife, which was an independent kingdom in the early Middle Ages, got its name from Fib, one of the seven sons of the Pictish king Cruithne, whose names were used in various place names throughout Scotland. The place name became a surname, and the surname in turn became an occasional first name, also found in the form **Fyfe**. Another legend, without substance, says that the surname marks a descendant of the younger son of Macduff, earl of Fife, so cruelly killed by Shakespeare's Macbeth.

Fingal *m.*

This name has been recorded from the early fourteenth century, but became famous when James Macpherson used it as the hero of his 'Ossian' poems in 1765. In 1832 the German composer Mendelssohn wrote his *Fingal's Cave* overture, inspired by Macpherson and the cave at Staffa. Macpherson's Fingal plays the part taken in Irish myth by the great hero **Finn**. **Fingall** is an alternative spelling, and the Gaelic form is **Fionnghall** meaning 'fair stranger', traditionally used to describe blond Vikings, while the dark ones were called DOUGAL. Fingal, although well known, is not a common name. However, it was the second name of Oscar Wilde.

Finlay *m.*

This is the anglicized form of the Gaelic name **Fionnlagh**, or in some dialects **Fionnla**, which comes from *fionn laoch*, 'fair hero', traditionally the name of Macbeth's father. It was a popular name, recorded from the earliest times, and also became one of the commonest Scottish surnames. **Findlay** is an old spelling, now mainly confined to the surname; **Finley** is also found.

Fiona f.

This name was formed from the Gaelic word *fionn*, 'fair, white'. It was used by James Macpherson in his Ossian poems, and was apparently his creation, for the -a ending is not a Gaelic one, though there are several similar ancient names. The name became popular after it was used as a pen name by William Sharp (1855–1905) for his alter ego the romantic poetess Fiona Macleod, and is still well used in Scotland as well as elsewhere. In recent years a number of spelling variants have occurred, such as **Fionna** and **Ffyonna**.

Forbes m.

This is an Aberdeenshire place name, now used as a surname and first name. It comes from Old Gaelic *forba-ais*, 'at the land or place'. It could be pronounced as two syllables until the beginning of the twentieth century.

Fraser m.

This name comes from a Norman surname first found in Scotland in the form *Frisel*, and also *de Fresel*, *de Friselle* and *de Freseliere*. The meaning of this name is not known. Because of a similarity of sound, the family adopted the strawberry plant, in French *fraisier* – hence **Frazier** – as its symbol, and this may have influenced the development of the modern form. The family became an exceedingly powerful and thoroughly Gaelic one. The surname became adopted as a first name, which is currently popular and also found in the alternative spelling **Frazer**.

F

Gavin m.

This is the Scottish form of the name more familiar to readers of Arthurian Romance as **Gawain**. In these romances Gawain is son of King Lot of Lothian, so the name has always had strong Scottish connections. A Scottish tradition makes Gawain himself king of Galloway. The source of the names is not clear. The early Welsh name for this character is *Gwalchmai*, 'Hawk of May', but it then appears in French as *Gauvin*, which then becomes **Gawan**, **Gawin** and Gavin in Scotland (as in the poet Gawin or Gavin Douglas (1475–1522). Gavin is steadily popular in Scotland and is found elsewhere in the English-speaking world.

Gilchrist m.

The Gaelic *gille* means a youth or servant, and is the source of the modern word *gillie*. In the early Middle Ages it was often attached to holy names to form new names, indicating that the bearer was a servant or a devotee of that particular saint. Thus Gilchrist (*Gille Chriosd*) was a devotee of Christ, **Gilleonan** (*Gille Adamhnain*) a devotee of St Adamnan (see ADAM), **Gillanders** (*Gille Anndrais*) a devotee of St Andrew and **Gillean** (*Gille Eoin*) a devotee of St John (source of the surnames Gilzean and MacLean). However, **Gillespie** (*Gille Easbaig*) was literally a servant of a bishop (see ARCHIBALD) and **Gilroy** (*Gille Ruaidh*) means 'red-haired boy'.

Giles m.

Giles comes from the name of a Greek saint, originally called Aegidius. This name was transformed into Giles in

France, where according to tradition he ended his days. He was a popular saint in Scotland, particularly in Edinburgh, where the High Kirk was dedicated to him. In the past Giles was used for both sexes, and there was a feminine form **Egidia**, which is mainly found in Scotland. This was, in fact, often a book form of the name, the name actually being pronounced 'Giles'. The female form of the name eventually became transformed into Julia or Juliana, while in Gaelic, which has no J, the name became **Sileas** (m.) or **Silis** (f.).

Gillies *m.*

This is one of the better-used *gille* names (see GILCHRIST), coming from the Gaelic **Gille Iosa**, 'servant of Jesus'.

Glen(n) *m. & f.*

This is a common Scottish surname, but qualifies as a Scottish first name only in that the word itself is Scottish. As a first name it is used in Scotland, but is more common in the USA and Canada, where it first rose to popularity. The forms **Glenna** and **Glenne** are also used for girls.

Gordon *m.*

This is a famous and important Scottish surname, used as a first name. The surname came from a Berwickshire place name, probably from the British meaning 'spacious fort'. It was rarely used as a first name until after 1885, when the dramatic death of General Gordon at Khartoum made the name popular both in Scotland and beyond.

Graeme, Graham *m.*

Graeme is currently the most popular spelling in Scotland of the first name that comes from the surname more frequently found as Graham. Rather surprisingly, the surname comes from Lincolnshire in England, probably the place now called Grantham. William de Graham was one of the Norman lords who accompanied DAVID I to Scotland and through marriage acquired land and power in Scotland. The spelling Graeme comes from a sixteenth-century story that the origin of the name came from a mythical Grim or Gram who broke through the Antonine Wall, built by the Romans, about 420 AD The spelling **Grahame** is also occasionally found.

Grant *m.*

This is a Scottish clan name currently a popular first name in Scotland. It comes from Norman-French *le grant*, 'big (man)', which would originally have been a nickname given to someone tall.

Gregor *m.*

This is the anglicized spelling of Gaelic **Griogair**, a form of the name **Gregory**. This is ultimately a Greek name, from the word meaning 'to be watchful', but was associated with the Latin work for 'flock, herd' and taken to refer to the Christian Good Shepherd. Because of this it became a popular name for early Christians and was chosen as a name by 16 Popes and a number of early Scottish bishops. In legend the name has been confused with the supposed King Giric or Griogar, a son of Kenneth MacAlpin. He was known to Medieval Chroniclers as 'Gregory the Great' and claimed as the

G

founder of the MacGregor clan. Gregor is currently quite a popular name in Scotland, but **Greg** is even more popular. This can be seen as a short form of Gregor, or from the surname Greg(g) or Greig, ultimately from the same source. The Norwegian composer Edvard Grieg was a descendant of a Scotsman of this name who had settled in Norway.

Griselda, Grizel f.

The name Griselda became a symbol of meek, patient womanhood in the Middle Ages after Boccaccio wrote the story of Patient Griselda, telling the story of a saintly woman who kept silent and obedient despite all the terrible things her husband did to her to test her. The story was translated into English by Chaucer, a poet greatly admired by Scots in the fifteenth century. In Scotland, Grizel became the standard form of the name, and was very popular. However, it is now rare.

G

Haki *m.*

Haki is an Orkney form of the Norse name Hakon. Hakon was a common name among the Norse settlers in Orkney, and was the name of one of its prominent earls, Hakon Paulsson. Haki was sometimes anglicized as **Hercules**, and this can occasionally still be found. Hercules is also said to be used for the Gaelic name **Athairne**.

Hamish *m.*

Hamish is the Anglicization of **Seumas** or **Sheumas**, the Gaelic forms of JAMES. Both Hamish and James, a biblical name of uncertain meaning and long-standing Scottish royal name, are still popular in Scotland.

Heather *f.*

As one of the plants most closely associated with Scotland, it is not surprising that this is a popular name with parents both in Scotland and of Scottish descent. The name first came into use towards the end of the nineteenth century.

Hector *m.*

Hector, meaning 'hold fast', and the name of the great hero of Troy, has long been a popular name in Scotland, recorded as early as 1369. Much of this popularity was because it was chosen to anglicize the Gaelic name **Eachan(n)**, which means 'horseman'. A famous holder of the name was Red Hector of the Battles, chief of the Macleans in the fifteenth century. Hector was shortened to **Heckie** or **Eckie**, and a feminine form, **Hectorina**, has been recorded.

H

Hugh *m.*

Hugh, though not a name commonly thought of as particularly Scottish, has had an important role in Scottish naming traditions. In origin it was a Germanic name, meaning 'mind, spirit', and has been used in Scotland since at least the twelfth century. It has also been used as the English equivalent of three different Gaelic names. It was used for **Aodh** 'fire' (see AIDAN), **Eòghann** (see EUAN) and for **Uisdean(n)**, which was a North-Western Gaelic name that was an adaptation of the Norse name *Eystein*, made up of elements meaning 'always, ever' and 'stone'. **Hughie** is a traditional pet form, and there was an old feminine, **Hughina**.

H

Iain, Ian m.

Iain is the original Gaelic form and currently the more popular spelling in Scotland of the name spelt elsewhere Ian. It is the Gaelic form of John, a biblical name meaning 'the Lord is gracious'. EOIN or **Eòin** is an alternative Gaelic form of the name. The Irish form of John, Sean or Shaun is currently popular in Scotland.

Ina f.

Because of the Scottish tradition of turning men's names into women's by adding the suffix -ina, and so producing names such as Adamina, Douglasina and Murdina, Ina has a particularly important role to play in Scottish names because it was the form these names were usually shortened to.

Inga f.

The Scandinavian settlers in the Northern and Western Isles, brought with them, before their conversion to Christianity, the worship of the fertility god Ing, and also the use of his name in various personal names. This can still sometimes be found in Shetland, most commonly in the shortened form Inga. In the past **Ingrid** was common. **Ingeborg** (**Ingibjorg**) was popular in Viking times and was the name of one of the most prominent women in the Saga of the Earls of Orkney, mother to two of the most famous earls and later wife of Malcolm King of Scots and mother to King Duncan.

Iona f.

This is an increasingly popular girl's name, taken from the holy island of Iona in the Hebrides. It was not much used, if at all, before the twentieth century. As a place name Iona comes from its Gaelic name *I*, itself an adaptation of the Old Norse word *ey*, 'an island'. The island's name was turned into *Ioua* in Latin, which was then misread as Iona. The island played an important role in early Scottish history. It was there that St Columba (see CALLUM) came in 563 to found the monastery from which Christianity spread to Scotland, and it was the burial place of Scotland's kings.

Irvine, Irving *m.*

These names both come from Scottish surnames derived from a place in Ayrshire, which got its name from the British *ir afon*, 'green water'.

Ishbel *f.*

Ishbel and the Gaelic **Iseaba(i)l** are Scottish forms of the name Isobel, in turn a form of Elizabeth, from the Hebrew 'oath of God'. Ishbel Gordon, Lady Aberdeen (1857–1939) was a great philanthropists and campaigner for women's rights, and Ishbel was also the name given to the daughter of Ramsey MacDonald, the first Labour prime minister. **Isbel** and the Gaelic pet form **Bealeag** (Bella) are also found.

Isla *f.*

Isla is the name of a river and glen in Perthshire, but because it is also represents the normal pronunciation of the Hebridean island of **Islay**, it may in fact come from that, particularly as Islay has been used as a first name for both sexes. The 's' is in both cases silent. The actresses, Isla St Clair and Isla Blair have made it better known.

Ivar, Ivor, Iver *m.*

Ivar (Gaelic **Imhaer** or **Iomhar**) was adopted as a
Scottish personal name in those areas which came under
Norse influence. It was a popular Norse name, coming
from words meaning 'yew' and 'warrior'. A Viking called
Ivar was a leader at the sack of Dumbarton in 870. Ivar
was a popular name among the Campbells, one of whom,
in the sixteenth century, was the progenitor of the
MacIvers. It was sometimes anglicized to **Evander**, the
name of a Greek demi-god who is supposed to have
founded a city in Italy.

1

James m.

The name of seven Stuart kings of the Scots, the last two were also kings of England, and of the latter's (James II) heir James Edward Stuart, known as the Old Pretender, was known by some as James III and VIII. The Latin form of the name James is *Jacobus* (Jacob), which is why the supporters of the last of the Stuart line were known as Jacobites, and also explains why **Jacobina** as well as **Jamesina** were names such supporters gave their daughters. The Gaelic forms of James developed into HAMISH. It has the usual short forms in Scotland as elsewhere, with one, **Jimmy**, being a common form of address in the Glasgow area.

Janet f.

Although it is now used as an independent name, Janet was originally a Scottish pet form of Jane, the feminine form of John from the Hebrew 'the lord is gracious'. The Gaelic form of Janet is **Seonaid**, which was anglicized to **Shona**, and there is a dialect form, **Deonaid**. Although it is itself a pet form, Janet was so popular that it developed its own pet forms. **Jessie** is a common one, and **Jenny** was used for Janet long before Jennifer became popular in the twentieth century. Less common is **Jinty**.

Jean f.

Like JANET, Jean is a Scottish form of Jane. **Jeanie** is a pet form, as is **Jess**, and it shares **Jenny** and **Jessie** with Janet. In Gaelic Jane or Jean becomes **Sine** (anglicized as **Sheena**), Jeanie becomes **Sineag** or **Sionag**, and Jessie, **Teasag**.

Jock *m.*

Jock is a Scottish pet form of the name **John**, the equivalent of the English Jack. Although it looks a long way from John, it comes from the affectionate ending -*kin* being added to John. The 'n' then dropped out of 'Jonkin' and the whole was shortened to leave 'Jock'. John has long been a popular name in Scotland – more than one in five soldiers in the Young Pretender's army in 1745 is recorded as a John (although this would have included those that called themselves IAIN) – and even today, when the name is in decline in other English-speaking countries, it is popular in Scotland. Jock is used as term for a Highland soldier, and outside Scotland more generally for a Scotsman. It has developed new pet forms **Jockie**, **Jockey** and **Jockan**, and is spelt **Seoc** and **Seocan** in Gaelic. John and Johnny become **Seathan** and **Seonaidh** in Gaelic.

J

Keir m.

A Scottish surname, which came from either the British or the Gaelic word for 'fort', used as a first name, principally in honour of (James) Keir Hardie (1836–1915), founder of the Scottish Labour Party and fighter for workers' rights.

Keith m.

Keith is from a Scottish surname from the British word for 'a wood' which came to be used for a first name. In the middle of the twentieth century it was popular throughout the English-speaking world, but it is not as well used now.

Kelvin m.

Kelvin is the name of a river that runs through Glasgow. It was taken for his title by the great Scottish scientist William Thompson, Lord Kelvin (1824–1907) when he was made a baron, after whom the Kelvin temperature scale is named. It has only been used as a first name since the twentieth century.

Kenneth m.

Kenneth MacAlpin, king of the Dalriada Scots of Western Scotland, conquered the Picts and made himself king of all the land north of the Forth, effectively the first king of Scots, in 843. The Gaelic form of his name is **Cinaed**, meaning 'born of fire'. Another Gaelic name **Coinneach**, 'handsome, fair one', is also anglicized as Kenneth. The name has the pet form **Kenny**, and feminine forms **Kenna** and **Kenina** have been recorded.

Kirsty *f.*

Also spelt **Kirstie** and in the Highlands **Chirsty**. This is the pet form of **Kirsten** or **Kirstin**, the Scottish form of Christine, both currently popular names with Scottish parents. In Gaelic the name is spelt **Curstaidh**, **Ciorstiadh**, **Curstag** or **Ciorstag**. The masculine form, Christopher, has an old pet form, **Kester**.

Kyle *m.*

As a surname, which became a first name, this comes from an area of Ayrshire named after a fifth-century king, Coel, who is also the origin of Old King Cole of nursery rhyme fame. The familiar use of Kyle as a geographic term for a narrow stretch of sea comes from a different source, the Gaelic *caol*, 'straits'. Although Kyle is currently popular with Scottish parents, its world-wide popularity is not a particularly Scottish phenomenon. There is a feminine form, **Kyla**.

K

Lachlan *m.*

This is a name we owe to the Norse inhabitants of the Western Isles, for it means 'fjord-land', i.e. Norway, and was originally given to immigrants from there. The Gaelic spelling is **Lachlann** or **Lachann**. It is shortened to **Lachie**, **Lacky** and **Lack**, and in Canada **Lockie**. There is a feminine form, **Lachina**. While it is still used in Scotland, it is not particularly popular, and is more likely to be found in families of Scottish descent in Canada and particularly Australia. General Lachlan Macquarie was Governor of New South Wales 1809–21, and gave his name to the style of architecture of the period.

Leslie, Lesley *m. & f.*

This comes from a Scottish surname, which in turn comes from a region in Aberdeenshire, of uncertain meaning, but possibly from the Gaelic for 'garden of holly'. The form Lesley was used in the late eighteenth century by Robert Burns for a woman to whom he addressed some of his poems. Originally, Leslie was used for men and Lesley for women, but Lesley is now occasionally used as a masculine, while both forms, with every additional spelling imaginable, are now used for women.

Lindsay *m. & f.*

This is a Scottish surname, of the earls of Crawford, which has become a first name. The first bearer of the surname was Walter de Lindsay, who was one of the Norman barons who came north with DAVID I. Although it may come from a Norman place name, it probably comes from the area around Lincoln, which ultimately goes back to a British name meaning 'the pools', which is recorded from Roman times. It came into general use as a first name in the 1930s, but is now little used for boys. As a girl's name it is found in a huge variety of spellings, including **Lindsey**, **Lynsay** and **Linzi**.

Logan *m.*

This is a place name, from the Gaelic word for a 'little hollow', which became first a surname and then a first name.

Lorne *m.*

A comparatively rare name, though born by the late actor Lorne Green, but an ancient one. Tradition as it that three Irish brothers, Fergus, Angus and Lorne settled in Dalriada about 500 AD. **Lorna** is not a traditional Scottish feminine form but seems to have been invented by R.D. Blackmoore for his 1869 novel *Lorna Doone*.

Ludovic *m.*

This Germanic name is still used in Scotland, where it came into use to anglicize **Maol Dòmhnaich**, 'devotee of the Lord'. The '-mhn-' part of this name is pronounced 'v' and the 'ch' as 'k', so the two names did contain the same sequence of sounds. Ludovic is shortened to **Ludo**.

L

Magnus *m.*

The name of the great eighth-century Emperor Charlemagne is just an adaptation of the Latin form of his name *Carolus Magnus*, 'Charles the Great'. The Scandinavians adopted the 'great' part of this, and Magnus became a popular name there. They took the name south with them when they occupied parts of Scotland. Magnus Barelegs, King of Norway ceded the Hebrides and Kintyre to the Scottish throne in 1098, having ruled them until then. In 1116 Magnus Erlendsson, Earl of Orkney was murdered by his cousin and co-ruler, praying for the souls of his killers all the while. He was canonized and the great cathedral at Kirkwall is dedicated to him. It is therefore not surprising that the name has been particularly popular in Orkney. The Gaelic form is **Mànas**.

Maisie *f.*

Maisie is a Scottish form of MARGARET, via **Marsaili** the Gaelic form of the pet form **Margery**. It is sometimes found in the form **Mysie**, and it has been suggested that **Maidie**, a name occasionally found in Scotland and Ireland, may come from it.

Malcolm *m.*

This comes from the Gaelic *Maol Coluim*, 'devotee of St Columba' (see CALLUM). It was the name of four kings, one of whom, Malcolm II, defeated the Lothian Angles in 1038. Another king, Malcolm III, known as Canmore ('big head'), was the son of DUNCAN. He defeated Macbeth in 1057, and was married to St MARGARET. **Malcolmina** and **Malina** are feminine forms.

Malvina f.

Also found as **Melvina** and **Malvena**, Malvina was a name invented by the Scottish poet James Macpherson (1736–96), for his Ossianic poems. These were works based on ancient material that Macpherson had gathered, and which received international acclaim when they were published in 1760s. Macpherson claimed they were translations of a Gaelic epic by Ossian, warrior-poet and son of the legendary hero FINGAL. The detection of the fact that much of the material was Macpherson's own invention has led to their neglect, but some of the names live on, especially in Scandinavia, where the poems were particularly influential. As well as Malvina, which may be based on the Celtic for 'smooth brow', there is **Morven** (f.), the name of Fingal's kingdom (modern north Argyll). This comes from the Gaelic for 'the big gap'. **Selma** (f.) was the name of Fingal's castle, and only became a personal name because of an ambiguity in the Swedish translation of the poems. **Morna**, 'beloved', was the name of Fingal's mother. It has been suggested that Malvina may the source of the masculine name **Melvin**.

Margaret f.

Although it is not a particularly popular name with Scottish parents at the moment, Margaret has a long history of use in the country, in honour of St Margaret (1046–93). She was a member of the deposed Anglo-Saxon royal family of England and was very influential in her husband's court. She never learnt Gaelic, and as a result the court became more anglicized. It was probably she who chose the then exotic names DAVID and ALEXANDER for two of her sons who later became kings. She was deeply devout and heavily influenced the church

in Scotland. In Gaelic Margaret becomes **Mairead** or
Mairghead, with pet forms **Magaidh** (**Maggie**) and
Peigi (**Peggy**). See also ETTA; MAISIE.

Maxwell *m.*

Maxwell, on the river Tweed, got its name from a Saxon
called Maccus who was granted the land by David I. The
family that took its name from the place rose to be earls
of Morton and Nithsdale, and became one of the leading
Jacobite families in the area. There has recently been
something of a fashion for using the surname as a first
name both in North America and the UK.

Mhairi *f.*

Mhairi is the Gaelic form of the name Mary, and is
currently very popular with Scottish parents. It is sometimes found as **Màiri**, and the equivalent of the pet form
Molly is **Màili**. The form of the name used for the
Virgin Mary is **Moire**, and from this has developed the
name **Moirean**.

Morag *f.*

Morag was originally a pet form of the Gaelic name
Mór, 'great, large'. It was popular earlier on in the
twentieth century, but is less common now. It has
traditionally been anglicized, for some unknown reason,
as Sarah.

Muireall *f.*

This is the Gaelic form of the name, found in all the
Celtic languages, meaning 'sea-bright' and is usually

anglicized as **Muriel**. **Mora(i)nn** is a related name, meaning 'sea-fair'.

Mungo *m.*

Mungo, said to mean 'beloved', was the pet name of St Kentigern, the evangelist of Strathclyde and patron saint of Glasgow. He seems to have been of British descent and a younger contemporary of St Columba, but the facts of his life are swamped by legend. The name is rare, but kept alive by the fame of the eighteenth-century Scottish missionary-explorer Mungo Park.

Murdo, Murdoch *m.*

This is the anglicized spelling of the Gaelic **Murchadh**, which comes from the Gaelic *muir* 'sea'. There are short forms, **Murdy**, **Murdie** and **Murdanie**, and the feminine forms **Murdag**, **Murdann**, **Murdina**, shortened to **Dina**, have been recorded. Murdoch, Duke of Albany was regent of Scotland during part of James I captivity in England, but was beheaded by James when he returned to Scotland in 1424.

Murray *m.*

This is a common Scottish surname used as a first name. It comes from **Moray**, meaning 'sea settlement', in north-east Scotland. The earls of Moray played a prominent part in Scottish history. Thomas Randolph, Earl of Moray was the nephew of Robert Bruce, and regent to Bruce's 5-year-old son David II, when he came to the throne in 1329. The Bonnie Earl of Moray of the well-known song was a popular Protestant lord, assassinated in the reign of James VI.

M

Neil *m.*

The story of the semi-legendary Irish hero Neal or **Niall** of the Nine Hostages, emphasizes the close connections between Ireland and mainland Britain. He was one of the most powerful Irish kings of his time, so powerful that nine other chiefs sent him hostages, but may himself had been half British. His mother was supposed to have been a British woman captured on a raid, and he himself frequently raided across the Irish sea for booty and captives to make slaves, one of whom may have been St Patrick. The name is also spelt **Neal**, and has a Scottish pet form **Neilie**, and a feminine **Neilina**. **Nigel** is also a form of Neil. For some unclear reason Latin scribes inserted a 'g' in their translations of the name into Latin, which was then retranslated back as Nigel. **Nigella** and **Nigelia** are feminine forms.

Nessa, Nessie *f.*

These are Scottish pet forms of the name Agnes (although nowadays sometimes used for Vanessa). Nessie is of course the affectionate nickname given to the Loch Ness Monster, just as MORAG is used of the similar animal said to live in Loch Mor. The name **Senga**, which had a brief flurry of popularity in Scotland in the mid-twentieth century, is said to come from Agnes spelt backwards.

Ninian *m.*

St Ninian, the meaning of whose name is not known, was a fourth-century Strathclyde Briton who converted the Picts and Britons to Christianity. He started his ministry in 397 or 389, basing it at Whithorn.

Archaeologists have found the remains of what appears to be his church. There are few hard facts about Ninian, but he appears to have been the child of Christian parents, which would indicate that the area was not entirely pagan before his time. **Ringan** is an Irish corruption of the name.

N

Ranulf *m.*

This is the Scottish form of the Old Norse name *Reginulfr*, which was formed from elements meaning 'advice' and 'wolf'. It was brought to Scotland by Viking settlers.

Robert *m.*

Robert, in origin a Germanic name formed from elements meaning 'famous' and 'bright', has long been a popular Scottish name. It was the name of one of the country's most famous kings Robert the Bruce (Robert I) who ruled 1306–29. **Rab** and **Rabbie** are distinctively Scottish short forms and it becomes **Raibeart** in Gaelic. Feminine forms have included **Roberta**, **Robina**, **Roby** and **Robena**.

Rona, Rhona *f.*

The origin of this name is a bit of a mystery. It appeared in Scotland in the 1870s, and may represent a feminine form of RONALD or RONAN or a form of Ragnhild (see RONALD). However, there is also an island between Skye and the mainland called Rona, 'rough island', and given that other islands in the area have been used as first names this may been a source.

Ronald *m.*

This is the commonest form of the many names that come from the Old Norse name *Rognvald*, formed from elements meaning 'advice' and 'ruler'. In the north of Scotland it was commonly used in the form **Ranald**, which along with Rognvald can still be found. The Gaelic form is **Raghnall**, and this is sometimes anglicized as **Randal**, as in the ballad 'Lord Randal'. There is a Gaelic variant, **Raonull**. Ultimately, **Reginald** and **Reynold** are from the same name. There is a feminine form of Ronald, **Ronalda**, and also a related female name, the Gaelic **Raghnaid** from Old Norse *Ragnhild*, formed from elements meaning 'advice' and 'battle'. Rognvald was a popular name in Viking Scotland, being borne among others by a king of the Hebrides, and Rognvald Kali Kolsonn, Earl of Orkney, who the sagas say travelled to Jerusalem and had dealings with the emperor of Byzantium.

Ronan *m.*

This is really an Irish name, meaning 'little seal', but various Irish saints of the name have connections with Scotland, particularly a seventh-century hermit who was supposed to have been 'tormented by the evil tongues of the women' of Eoroby on the island of Lewis, and to have been taken by a whale to the island of North Rona, where he built a chapel whose ruins can still be seen. **Ronat** (**Ronnat** or **Ronait**) is an Irish feminine form of the name.

Rory *m.*

Rory or **Rorie** is the anglicized form of the Gaelic *Ruairi(dh)* or *Ruaraidh*, meaning 'red king'. The name was also anglicized as **Roderick**, and developed the feminine forms **Rodina** and **Rhoda**.

Ross *m.*

Ross is a common British place name, meaning either 'headland' or 'wood', which became both a widespread surname and a clan name. It has a long history of use as a first name both in Scotland and Ireland, and is currently one of the most popular choices with Scottish parents.

Roy *m.*

Roy comes from the Gaelic **Ruad**, meaning 'red', and was originally a nickname for someone with red hair. It gained fame as the name of Rob Roy Macgregor (1671–1734), outlaw and adventurer, and to some the Scottish Robin Hood; particularly after a romantic version of his life was published as a novel by Sir Walter Scott in 1818.

R

Scott *m.*

This is a surname used as a first name. Although it is obviously Scottish in origin, it first became popular as a first name in the USA. Influenced, at least in part, by the fame of the author F. Scott Fitzgerald. However, it has been a popular name in Scotland for some years. It is among the 10 most common Scottish surnames, and would originally have been given to a Gaelic speaker living in a non-Gaelic area. The Scots were originally a northern Irish tribe who settled in the Western part of Scotland in the Dark Ages, and whose spreading influence throughout the country can be traced in the history of the names in this book.

Sholto *m.*

A name quietly but steadily used, particularly in the Douglas family. It's origin is not entirely clear, but it appears to come from the Gaelic *Sioltach*, meaning 'sower, fruitful'.

Skye *m. & f.*

The name of the Hebredean island used as a first name, in the same way that IONA is. It is quite a recent introduction to the list of first names, but it's use has been growing steadily in recent years, particularly in the USA. It is more common for it to be used as a girl's name rather than a boy's. The name of the island is very ancient, and is recorded from Roman times. It's name is probably connected with the Gaelic word *sgian*, 'knife', best known from the *sgian-dubh*, the black knife worn in the stocking in full Highland dress, and may refer to the deep cuts in the coastline

Sorcha f.

This Gaelic name, best known Ireland, but used in Scotland as well, comes from a word meaning 'brightness'. This has led to it's being anglicized in Scotland as Clara, which has the same meaning, though in Ireland it usually becomes Sarah.

Sorley m.

This name can still be found in its old form **Somerled**, from an Old Norse nickname meaning 'summer-traveller' given to someone who spent his summers as a Viking raider. It became a popular name with descendants of Viking settlers, among whom was Somerled Lord of Argyll – or as he preferred it King of Morven, Lochaber, Argyll and the Southern Hebrides – who sacked Glasgow in 1153. As the Norse settlers were absorbed into the Gaelic population the name became **Somhairle** in Gaelic. It is this form that is anglicized to **Sorley**. It has gained fame in recent years as the name of the great Gaelic poet Somhairle MacGill-Eain, or in English translation, Sorley Maclean.

Struan m.

This is the place name Strowan or Struan in Perthshire, used as a first name. Strowan was long the home of the chiefs of the Robertson clan, and therefore the name is particularly used by that family.

Stuart, Stewart m.

Walter FitzAlan, Hereditary High Steward of Scotland, also known of Walter the Steward, or Walter Stewart, married Margery, daughter of Robert Bruce. In 1333 their son, Robert, then 17, became the regent for his 10-year-old uncle, David II. On David's death Robert was then elected king as Robert II – the first Stewart king. The royal surname name did not become used as a first name until the nineteenth century. It is found in the original spelling and in the French form used by Mary Queen of Scots, Stuart. Both are popular names in Scotland at the moment, with Stuart the preferred spelling. A rarer variant is **Steuart**, and the name becomes **Stiubhart** in Gaelic.

S

Tam *m.*

This is the particularly Scottish form of Tom, well known from Burns's 'Tam o' Shanter'. In Gaelic Thomas becomes **Tòmas** or **Tàmhas**. This last form gave rise to a surname, MacThàmas, 'son of Thomas', which was anglicized as MacTavish, giving rise to the occasional use of **Tavish** as a first name. **Tòmachan** and **Tòmag** are Gaelic pet forms of Thomas.

Thora *f.*

Thora is an Old Norse name based on the Viking thunder god Thor. It was used in the Orkneys, where Thora Sumarlidi's daughter was the mother of St MAGNUS.

Torquil *m.*

The Old Norse name *Thorketill*, probably meaning 'Thor's (sacrificial) cauldron', was introduced to Scotland by the Viking settlers and became **Torcall** in Gaelic, which in turn was anglicized as Torquil. Thor was a particularly popular god. Records from Iceland show that he was not only associated with thunder, but was something of a patron god of farmers, and one of the most widely worshipped of the gods among Viking settlers. This gave rise to a number of personal names involving his name, some of which are still in occasional use. **Thurston** comes from 'Thor's stone'; **Tormod** or **Tormailt**, commonly anglicized as Norman, comes from Thor and an element meaning 'mind, courage'; **Turlough**, **Turley** or **Turloch**, in Gaelic **Teàrlach**, and familiar to readers of T.H.White in the old Irish spelling *Toirdhealbhach*, whichs was the name of the wild hermit who told stories to Gawain, Gareth, Agravain and Mordred in Book Two of *The Once and Future King*, and is traditionally thought of as coming from Thor, although this is now doubted; **Turval** comes from a name formed from Thor and 'ruler'. Also related to Torquil is **Taskill** (Gaelic **Tasgall**) which comes from Old Norse *Asketill*, 'god's cauldron'.

ᛏ

Wallace *m.*

This is a Scottish surname which has come to be used in honour of the great Scottish patriot and warrior William Wallace (c.1270–1305). As a surname it comes from the same Old English word that is the origin of the word Welsh, which meant 'foreign', and was used to indicate the native British people that the Saxons found in the country when they arrived. William Wallace's ancestors were probably Strathclyde Britons. The alternative spelling **Wallis** is occasionally found.

Wullie *m.*

This is the distinctively Scottish pet form of William, made famous by the cartoon character Oor Wullie. He has been appearing in the *Scottish Sunday Post* since 1934, and for many he has come to represent all that is best about everyday Scottish life. William has been a popular name in Scotland since the early Middle Ages, and takes the form **Uilleam** in Gaelic.

Index

Ealasaid see Ailsa
Eckie see Hector
Edan see Aidan
Edmé(e) see Esmé
Edom see Adam
Egidia see Giles
Eneas see Angus
Eoghann see Euan
Eoin see Iain
Eppie, Erica see Effie
Eunan see Adam
Euphame, Euphemia see Effie
Evander see Ivar

Fanny see Effie
Fearghas see Fergus
Finella, Finola, Fionola, Fionnghal Flora, Florrie, Floraidh see
Fenella

Gillanders, Gille Ainndreis, Gille Anndrais see Andrew
Gillespie, Gilleasbaig see Archibald

Hercules see Haki

Imhaer, Iomhar see Ivar
Innes see Angus

Jenny, Jess, Jessie see Janet, Jean
Jinty see Janet
Katriona, Katrina see Catriona
Kentigern see Mungo

MacBeth see Bean
Magaidh, Mairghead, Mairead see Margaret
Màili, Màiri see Mhairi
Maol Coluim see Malcolm
Maol Dòmhnaich see Ludovic
Maretta, Marietta see Etta
Marsaili see Maisie
Moirean see Mhairi
Morna, Morven see Malvina

Mysie see Maisie

Nigel, Nigelia, Nigella see Neil

Oighrig see Effie

Peigi see Margaret

Phemie see Effie
Rab, Rabbie see Robert
Raghnaid, Raghnall, Ranald, Randal, Raonull see Ronald
Raibert see Robert
Rhoda see Rory
Rhona see Rona
Ringan see Ninian
Roderick, Rodina, Ruairi(dh), Ruaraidh see Rory

Sandy, Sandaidh, Saunders, Sawney see Alexander
Seathan, Seonaidh see Jock
Selma see Malvina
Senga see Nessa
Seoc, Seocan see Jock
Seonaid see Janet
Seonaidh see Jock
Seumas see Hamish
Sheena see Jean
Sheumas see Hamish
Shona see Janet
Sileas, Silis see Giles
Sine, Sineag, Sionag see Jean
Somerled, Somhairle see Sorley

Tasgall, Taskill, Teàrlach see Torquil
Teasag see Jean
Tòmachan, Tòmag, Tòmas see Tam

Uilleam see Wullie

Uisdean(n) see Hugh
Vida, Vina see David, Davina

COLLINS

Other titles in *The Scottish Collection* series include:

ISBN 0 00 472326 0

ISBN 0 00 472325 0

ISBN 0 00 472304 X

Classic Malts   *Scottish Verse*   *Scottish Recipes*

Homelands of the Clans